On Matthew's Mind
6th Edition

This publication is designed to provide general information regarding the subject matter covered. However, laws and practices often vary from state to state and are subject to change. Because each factual situation is different, specific advice should be tailored to the particular circumstances. For this reason, the reader is advised to consult with his or her own advisor regarding each specific situation.

The author and publisher have taken reasonable precautions in the preparation of this book and believe the facts presented within are accurate as of the date it was written. However, neither the author nor the publisher assumes any responsibility for any errors or ommissions. The author and publisher specifically disclaim any liability resulting from the use or application of the information contained in this book, and the information is not intended to serve as legal, financial, or other professional advice related to individual situations.

Assisting, advising and consulting America's premier independent financial advisors. Services include (but are not limited to) business planning, analysis, management, organization, marketing and customer analysis.

Printed in the United States of America.

Copyright © 2017
Matthew J. Neuman
All rights reserved.

On Matthew's Mind
6th Edition

With hope for our futures Nico — individually and collectively.

Want more? Lean Into Matthew

www.matthewneuman.com

Twitter @matty_neu

866.363.9595

matt@advisorsexcel.com

2016 THOUGHTS

2016. Wow, what a year. Exhale.

It was the year of Trump, Hillary and the strangest United States Presidential election ever. Night after night, month after month on channel after channel, the barrage of messaging around these people was non-stop! Would it ever end?

2016 will also be remembered as the year of the Department of Labor (DOL) Fiduciary Rule, asking the nation's top financial advisers to innovate and improve. The ruling has aimed to stop $17 billion a year in what the government claims as investors waste on unnecessary fees. They believe their added regulation will mandate that client's interests will always come before advisers, and earning high commissions and fees will no longer lead the any part of the sales process. The nation's thousands of brokerage firms, insurance networks and advisory practices that give advice to a $25 trillion (with a "T") retirement market will have to adjust their operations and procedures, fundamentally shifting the future. How will the rubber hit the road? That part is yet to be seen.

But one thing is for certain as 2016 closes, and that's Americans continue to retire in droves. To be more specific, approximately 10,000 Americans are retiring every day, projected to continue for the next 15 years! If that wasn't enough, their investment choices and the multitude of professionals vying for attention all continue to broaden. Make no mistake about it, they need **your** help, **your** empathy, **your** expertise and grit more than ever. This is more than just your success.

So take solace knowing what you hold in your hands is genuine. It's authentic. It has the potential to inspire action, add significant revenue to your firm, drastically enhance the value of your business and substantially improve the lives of your clients for decades to come. Don't just skim, and then allow it to collect dust; **you deserve better...**

BIOGRAPHY

In consulting over a hundred of the most elite financial practitioners in the nation, Matthew Neuman is considered one of the most successful annuity professionals in todays marketplace. His empathy and passion proves time-and-time again to take those already great and lead them down a path to become legendary. Matthew's genuine approach makes the complex creation, sales and marketing of annuities and turns them into customized strategies for the best in the business.

As Advisors Excel's most tenured Vice President, Matthew has played an integral role in the firm's unprecedented success. By all accounts, Advisors Excel is the industry's most dominant insurance marketing distribution company ever. The firm's combined expertise helped Advisors Excel retire the Senior Market Advisor Reader's Choice Awards, become the first marketing organization to surpass $5 billion in annual annuity production *(with no end in sight)* and create, exclusively distribute and oversee two of the best selling FIAs in history!

Matthew currently serves on Senior Market Advisor's Advisory Board and regularly consults with Innovation Design Group, AgenciesHQ, Meek Rainey Group, The Annexus Group and Market Synergy Group. He is also the author of multiple sales pieces published nationwide, creator of the Custom Fit Calendar™ and posts candid, thought-provoking ideas to a dedicated band of followers on his blog at www.matthewneuman.com. Having graduated Cum Laude from Washburn University School of Business with honors in Management, Matthew brings a clear-cut blend of academic and real world insight to the partners he's alongside.

Outside of work, Matthew is devoted to an amazing family – with his wife Alice, and young boys Noah, Evan & Theo. He spends regular time fulfilling a life of faith and enjoys staying physically active through the "Sport of Fitness" as a CrossFit Level 1 (CF-L1) Trainer and completing endurance races, with a lifetime goal of completing an event in all 50 states.

Lastly, Matthew takes tremendous pride in having established the Neuman Family Fund with his wife in 2011. Since inception, Family Fund grants have totaled over $250,000, supporting a range of worthy causes in Northeast Kansas. The Neuman Family Fund continues to grow and plans to support efforts that empower and enlighten the local community and, in order to do so, need financial support, caring contributors and strategic guidance. They make regular grants from the Family Fund and are always on the lookout for worthwhile causes.

1ST TOOTH MOMENT

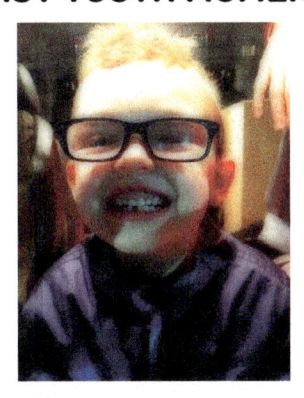

"Now that my first tooth is out, I feel a lot stronger dad. Like I can do more push-ups. And I even pulled the drain plug in my bath with only one hand tonight!"

That's what my son Noah told me a couple nights ago; less than twenty four hours after losing his first tooth. It's funny. Losing just one baby tooth has Noah looking at himself like the bigger, stronger kids in his Kindergarten class.

His state of mind, perspective and self-image has shifted.

I saw it professionally this week too. One of my newer producers I consult (from New Jersey) is finishing his first full year under our consultation. Over that time his self-image has changed dramatically. And while I haven't pinpointed his "First Tooth Moment" yet, I can lock down the source of his success. Over the last 10 months, Bill's transitioned from someone who apologized too often and looked at the floor too much into a confident, proud, assertive professional who just tripled his best year ever. And on pace to double his practice again next year!

State of mind and self-confidence are king.

So where are you headed into the new year?
What story's running through your mind?

Stuart Smalley motivation aside, you KNOW you have everything it takes to crush your goals, right? Create your own "First Tooth Moment", new connection, belonging or breakthrough if you must. Or simply start telling yourself a more assertive story. But whatever it takes, get it done.

It's go time; no excuses.

COMPANY CULTURE

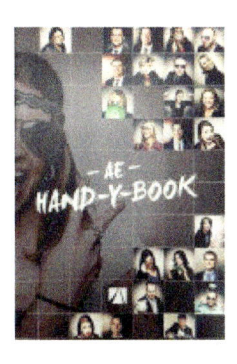

With the amount we travel, it made sense to get TSA pre-checked status done recently. Have you done that yet? Faster lines at airport security, less restrictions and less hassle. What's not to love?

Well...one thing's not to love...the process to get approved.

(I'm sure you've been here before too). Walking into the application facility, I was greeted by no one. No receptionist, no "hello" and no warm smile. Instead I was looking at a sign-in sheet, dirty chairs in a gathering area and three other bored-to-death men staring at their shoes. After a few minutes, a woman appeared behind the counter, looked at the clipboard and mumbled my name. She then walked me to a back room that couldn't have been more soulless had it tried. White-painted, cinder block walls, folding chairs, name badges, a bad cat calendar in the background, ten impersonal questions on a screen and four sets of fingerprints later; I was gone. Leaving the TSA pre-check facility, I thought about "work" and what it'd feel like entering that environment every morning.

AE Handy BookThe very next day, an opposite experience grabbed me. A thought leader I follow suggested I Google "Valve employee handbook" and what I found was inspiring and refreshing. (Later I discovered this manual is inspiration for the

Advisors Excel's internal "AE Handy-Book" that circulates around our office).

Valve is an entertainment software and technology company, and their employee handbook genuinely celebrates a unique company culture. At the very beginning of it, Valve guides their employees through:

"A fearless adventure in knowing what to do when no one's there telling you what to do."

And goes on to says their handbook is:

"...for new employees. Congratulations, and welcome. We want to make sure that your first experiences in our unique culture are easy to navigate—working without bosses, no one telling you what to work on next, what's the deal with the weekly massages, why do all the desks have wheels? What happens after you get here is something we spend a lot of time thinking about, so we've created a handbook for new employees that explains how we're organized (or not!), why we're set up that way, and what to expect the first day, first month, and first six months."

Without babbling on the wrap-up point, you know where we're headed...

Which of these 2 firms (TSA PreCheck or Valve) would you want to be part of?
If I asked your employees, which do you more represent?
If I asked your clients, which more describes the "feel" of your practice?
Lastly, how can you take from Valve and improve your company culture?

LET 'EM LOOSE

Some families show up at my son's school looking perfect.

Kid's hair styled, shoes cleaned, stains removed. And while I can appreciate those families, more power to 'em...**That's not us**.

Our boys are overly-loved and very well cared for. But our car being clean as they get dropped off, or their clothes matching, those are the least of my concerns. On the contrary. If choosing their owns clothes brings a self-confident smile to their face, that's what we're going to do!

Which has me thinking about you and your staff.

Those people who support you every day, the people you poured yourself into just before and right after hiring them. Do you hover over those people, trying to create perfection around every item they touch? Are you controlling to a level where they never feel free to step into their own shoes and **own** the work they produce? You're probably saying,

"Oh no. Not me. I'd never do that."

But if you think hard, on certain levels you do. I do. Because anyone with a hired team, "controls" their success to a certain extent & we can all do better.

That line between "leadership" and "hovering" can become easily blurred if we're not careful.

But the best know we need to let 'em loose. For everyone to achieve at the highest levels & feel satisfaction up Maslow's hierarchy, leaders MUST give up control. You need to have faith in your training, in your culture, in your processes and hiring decisions. **Then let everyone own their piece.** If you have the right people on board, you'll be amazed at what happens.

This coming from a guy who "dresses" his kids in denim shirts, gym shorts and cowboy boots.

MARKETING MANAGER

Does this make sense to you?

Someone spends $100,000, $200,000 or $300,000 a year to market new clients into their firm. But when I ask basic marketing return on investment, cost of client acquisition and budgeting questions, they're at a loss for words. Why? Because they're "too busy" to know. That's crazy.

One of the most successful advisors I've ever met told me,

"Know your numbers, know your business.

Don't know your numbers, no business."

Chew on this. If you're spending big money towards new client acquisition, you've already made the toughest decision. For that, I applaud you. You believe in yourself and are backing it up. But moving forward, be smart about it. What other successful, long-term focused business (not successful salesperson, but successful business) would spend that kind of money, yet not run tight tracking on results?

I'm not suggesting you step away from meeting with clients to crunch numbers and move marketing dials. After all, you're probably best when you're face to face, belly to belly, with the people who need your help. But what could a marketing manager do for your firm? Depending on your part of the country, that full time professional will "cost" you $40-$120,000 per year. **Is it worth it?**

Yes. Yes. Yes. If you're spending significant money to attract new clients, there is zero doubt a marketing manager is worth the money.

1. They'll take weight off your shoulders and allow you to focus where you shine most. That allows you to convert more often, run more meetings and generally smile more.

2. They can take the marketing money you're already spending and maximize it. They'll stay on top of tasks like tracking, ROI, budget movements and deployments, leads that fall through the cracks, drips between meetings and creating the BEST client culture around. All this leads to more success.

3. They can take over opportunities you're currently missing. Think about current client events to prompt more revenue and higher retention, think professional referral sources you're not taking time to approach and think charitable opportunities for your firm just to name a few.

What would it take to break even with that marketing director's pay? How many additional assets? And how much stress relief and excitement does it create as well? You're now able to move into the future and take advantage of everything you learn! **You'll be proactively planning instead of reactively responding.**

Know your numbers, know your business. Time to make that happen.

PERCEPTION & REALITY

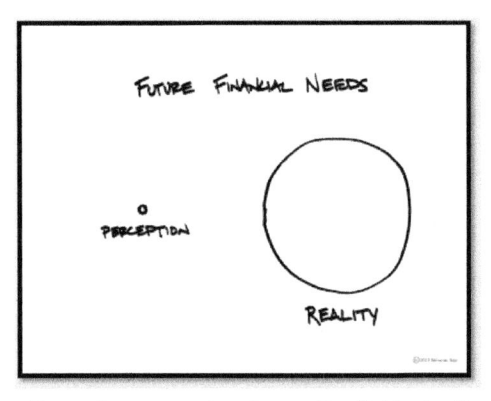

[Figure: hand-drawn chart titled "FUTURE FINANCIAL NEEDS" showing a small dot labeled "PERCEPTION" and a large circle labeled "REALITY"]

An old boss used to tell me **"perception is reality"**. I hate that.

Even worse, in showing his true (lack of) character, most times the next thing said was **"a lie stuck to is as good as the truth."** I'm not making this up. He meant it tongue-in-cheek funny, but after hearing those phrases numerous times, it was obvious they were internalized inside him.

Let's take those thoughts into the money world…

Ask anyone for an estimate of their future financial needs and the number you get is usually underestimated. Is their perception a reality? Is the lie they're sticking to as good as the truth? Emphatically – no.

Want some evidence? Check out "Retirement Reality: 8 Charts You Need to See" from Retirement Cheat Sheet. Once you combine most people's:

* Real savings rate
* Rising life expectancy
* Saving's lifespan
* Spending habits
* Potential nursing home expense
* Potential for additional Social Security changes

* Investing rate of return &

* Market timing

Things can get crazy in a hurry.

So what should they do? What can you help them do? Let me suggest something very simple:

1. Recognize if they have an issue
2. Internalize the importance of taking action and addressing it
3. Trust a knowledgeable and experienced financial professional (know anyone like that?) who can put together a personalized, tailored strategy.

These issues aren't going anywhere. Help people recognize that and take action. That's what you're best at.

THIN SLICING

My boys love French toast. Bread, butter, powdered sugar, the works if we let 'em. Saturday mornings kick start the best when Noah & Evan get tried-and-true French toast to fuel the weekend!

And when mom, dad or a restaurant prepares their French toast, we don't need anything fancy. The original recipe has worked for years and (unless something drastic changes) will stay that way. But that doesn't mean we can't take a small slice (thin slice if you will) of that bread loaf and try something new. Something creative, right? Maybe stuff a piece or two with cream cheese? Bake it in the oven? Cut it into shapes? Or integrate fruit somehow?

Just like your marketing.

You know what's tried and true. You know what works and needs repeated over and over with 90% of your bread loaf. But don't let it get old or boring. To stay ahead of the marketplace and fuel your innovation, I'll challenge you to thinly slice. Take 10% of your marketing budget and try a different mailer, different mail list, different event venue, different medium to use. It's fun, it's profitable, it's trend-setting and it keeps you feeling alive.

Want a couple pieces of our famous French toast? Sure.

But also try a couple bites of the newest twist we thought up last week!

MONEY MAKES YOU...

One of my top clients, and now closest friends, is crossing over our 10 year anniversary working together. She's an inspiration to me in a lot of ways – professional and personal.

First and foremost, thank you Sandy. Thank you for choosing me, for choosing us, and for leaning into our relationship this last decade.

Rewind back to 2009; when we asked Sandy to speak from stage. She was a superstar with us and open to paying back into the model, so it made sense.

While I'm not sure if she remembers what the talk was about, I certainly do. The first concept Sandy spoke about was **"relaxed intensity"**. It's a concept I loved that day and strive to embody myself (maybe a future blog post there).

But the second topic was on money; and what it does to you.

Sandy's always been successful, before I knew her and ever since. She's thrived at a very high level; and has achieved so much because of her contribution to others and the impact she's made across the United States. For that, Sandy's been rewarded monetarily and in life's experiences. And on that topic, from stage back in 2009, she told us how she viewed money. To Sandy, money:

1. Gives you comfort

2. Gives you choices

3. And beyond that – **Money makes you more of who you are**

* If you're greedy, money will make you more so.
* If you're unethical, money will bend those rules further.
* If you're grateful; that spirit of love and gratitude will shine brighter.
* If you're giving, your reach will grow wider and deeper.
* If you're self-centered, your focus will heighten inward.
* If your values are centered on family or faith; possessions or recognition, they will strengthen regardless.

Money makes you more of who you are.

And today I'm grateful for Sandy's friendship and wisdom.

HARD WORK (IN PERSPECTIVE)

What we do every day isn't hard work.

At 4 am today I greeted the Kansas City airport parking maintenance man. He was doing hard work. The line cook at McDonald's I see arriving at 5 am to prep burgers, that's hard work. The roofer, brick mason, warehouse stocker, farmer, assembly line worker – all those people perform hard work.

* Is hard work the same as smart work? **Often.**
* Is smart work the same as hard work? **Sometimes.**
* Is our (your) work important? **Absolutely.**
* Is our (your) work impactful? **Undoubtedly.**

Because every time I see a hard worker (particularly one smiling and pleasant) it puts my professional contribution in check. We love what we do. And I wouldn't change it for the world. But as we exhale from "exhaustion" at home each night, let's keep it in perspective.

1-2-3 PYRAMID

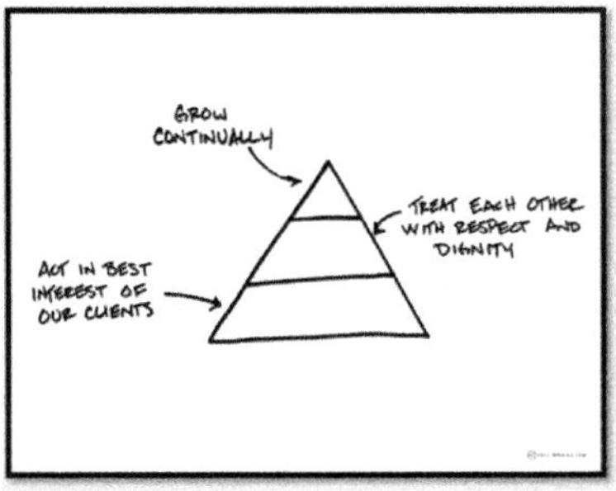
GROW CONTINUALLY
TREAT EACH OTHER WITH RESPECT AND DIGNITY
ACT IN BEST INTEREST OF OUR CLIENTS

Put client interests first. Always.

Treat people how they deserve to be treated.

Grow continually. *(You're either growing or dying, there is no "maintaining".)*

What else do you need?

With foundations like that set inside your firm, every future decision in the future becomes clear.

Now get to work defining **your own foundational principles** – stealing these or not. Next, tell them to your clients. They want and deserve to know what you're about.

MEANT TO BE

Noah: "Dad, I want to go on the Winnie the Pooh Ride."
Me: "Winnie the Pooh? Really? You haven't seen any of that stuff. You sure?"
Noah: "Yeah, I'm sure."
Evan: "Yeah, me too daddy."

So on our final day at Walt Disney World, we head into "The Many Adventures of Winnie the Pooh". Thrilling. At least it was early in the morning, so the wait wasn't long. Maybe 15 minutes and we were onto honey pots, donkeys in the rain and my two boys smiling ear to ear. As it's over we exit the ride, walk towards the (mandatory) Pooh gift shop and head for our next spot. But then, in one of those memorable moments, something happened that I'll never forget.

As we're moving through the gift shop my wife Alice spots something on the floor. "What is that?" she asks, and bends down to pick up a small piece of folded-up paper on the floor.

To really understand this, you'd have to know about our night before. We were at the hotel, planning our final Walt Disney World day and appreciating the fact that we'd been able to experience nearly everything we wanted – except one thing. The newest ride at Magic Kingdom was called "Seven Dwarfs Mine Train" and it looked incredible. Both of my sons (even the 2 ½ year old) were tall enough to ride it; and boy did they ever want to! This would be their first real roller coaster.

The problem? Every time we looked at wait times for "Seven Dwarfs Mine Train" it looked like this (screen shot from my iPhone that day):

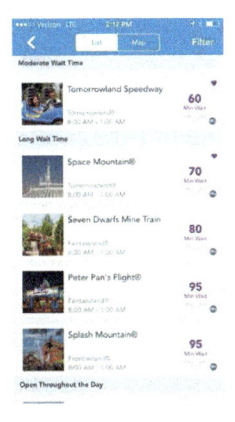

Were we going to wait in line an hour and a half, with two young boys in tow, for that ride? Some might, but we made the decision; no. It simply wasn't worth it.

Come back with me to "The Many Adventures of Winnie the Pooh" gift shop. Remember a folded-up piece of paper caught our eye and we just picked it off the floor.

Unfolding the paper, what was it?!? Here, let me show you (again, actual picture):

That can't be right, can it? It's a **"Fast Pass" (for the non-Disney initiated, that means permission to skip the line)** ticket, available to use that day for the "Seven Dwarfs Mine Train". Huh?

21

How could that be? How serendipitous, fortunate, lucky was that? It still blows my mind that we were then able to take that small piece of paper to the front of the line for one of the most memorable rides we had at Disney. Ask my boys next time you see them what they're favorite ride at Disney was and you're sure to hear about the "Seven Dwarfs Mine Train"!

So what's my point?

Maybe something along the lines of if it's meant to be, it'll happen. Or maybe something like it pays to be good AND lucky. Or maybe you just control what you can control and surrender the outcome.

I don't really know if I have a point. Other than wanting to share an incredible story that I'll never forget; knowing something beyond my understanding happened. I guess, if it's meant to be...

Has anything like this ever happened to you? Something unexplainable, magical, beyond logic? I'd love to hear about it.

SEND ME SOME INFO

Ugh!

If the #1 worst thing to hear in sales is **"Let me think about it"**, #2 is undoubtedly **"Send me some info."** And the only reason it's #2 instead of #1 is because you're hearing no earlier in the relationship.

Here's my suggestion...

NEVER accept those statements. NEVER move forward with sending that info (or letting them think about it) as if it's normal. The *"some will, some won't, so what, next"* attitude needs left in the 90's.

We all know those two phrases are simply canned, quasi-polite ways of someone shutting you down. I guess you could accept it. Then what? Feel discouraged and not engage again? Turn it into an uncomfortable sales pressure filled back and forth? And the whole time have angst in your mind?

Instead of accepting **"Send me some info"**, can we simply breathe, pause and ask a more sincere question to the human being we're visiting with? This isn't perfect, you need to make things natural for you, but what about this response?

"I can send anything you'll genuinely read that'll help. That's not a problem. But usually when someone says 'send me some information' they're politely saying 'I'm not interested'. I don't know if that's what you're telling me or not. So instead of sending information you probably won't read, then trying to reconnect again; on a person to person level, can you tell me what you're really thinking right now?"

Sales should be less about "sales". Embrace genuine conversation and treating people the way you'd like to be treated. Then never worry on people thinking about it or sending some information again.

BILLIONAIRES W/ 6-PACK ABS

Knowledge is power. Right?

Wrong. If that were the case, we'd all be billionaires with 6-pack abs.

Want proof? Here – **30.2 million**, followed by **14.5 million** results!

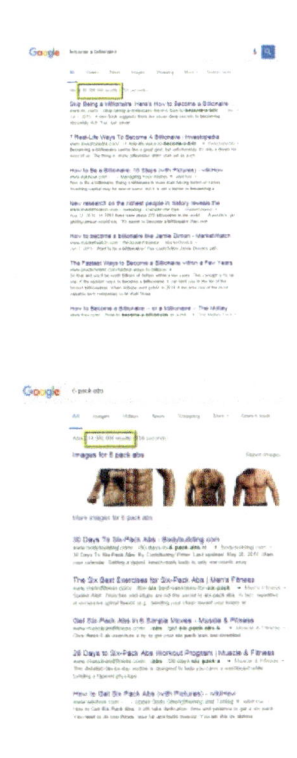

Knowledge without action is pointless.

The world belongs to "doers".

So keep learning, but do something with it. Or don't. Or do. Or don't. But I know I will.

LONG TERM AVERAGE

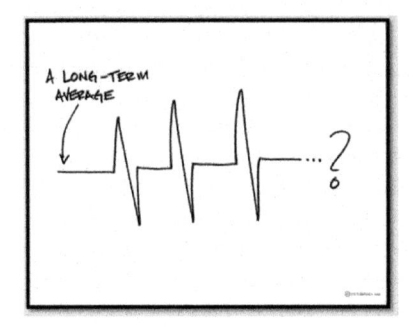

Up, down, flat.

Up, down, flat.

Up, down, flat.

Now what?

The cycle repeats itself, but no one is smart enough to know when (or why). Good luck.

DEATH TO POWERPOINT

With your public speaking, do you need PowerPoint?

No. Emphatically no. No. No.

- Quit lying to yourself.
- Grow into the here and now.
- Start believing in **your story and value**.
- Quit PowerPoint. Forever. You're better than that.

WHO DOES THIS? [PPI]

This morning a UPS envelope showed up on my desk.

Tearing it open, inside I found two things: a note card, and a Topeka Owls shirt. What in the world?!? The handwritten note was from Ann, one of my best clients and now closest friends. Ann wrote:

"Matt,

While in Haitt Ashbury w/ my daughter recently we came across the coolest t-shirt shop. Everything from Bob Marley to Metallica to the Topeka Owls?!? Who knew? Anyway, I thought of you and thought you'd be a conversation starter at the gym with this on."

How cool is that?!?

First, this is someone thinking of me while she's with her family in San Francisco. Second, she knows I played a lot of baseball growing up. And third, she knows I'd wear something like this to the gym in the morning.

NOW MY QUESTION: ARE YOU DOING THIS?

Are you doing this for your employees? Are you doing this for your clients? Your prospects? Are you doing things like this for your other business partners, so they view you differently?

Here inside my office we've formalized this informal, heartfelt process and called it PPI (Personalized, Positive Impact). And believe it or not, all 375 employees at our firm have a $50 monthly budget to make that happen. We're on the lookout for places to make an impact: every call, every email, every touch point of our relationship.

It's your turn now to make this happen. Do it personally and with staff inside your office. It's too fun not to.

(And thank you again Ann).

TOO SIMPLE

[Graph: Effectiveness vs. Simplicity, showing an upward curve]

One of the most brilliant financial advisers in the country tells me all the time:

"A confused mind says no."

He possesses more financial competence than nearly anyone I know. His prospects know that too; that's why they're sitting with him. But in guiding their financial lives, what if he drew something like this:

[Complex mathematical formulas]

(SOURCE: HTTP://WWW.FRUGALDAD.COM/SIMPLE-FORMULA-FOR-ACHIEVING-FINANCIAL-INDEPENDENCE/)

Could he? Sure.

Should he? No.

Instead he puts a prospective client's entire financial plan onto three pieces of paper. And he walks them through those three pages, asking the individual to make **one decision at a time**. After they make one decision at a time, 8 or 10 times, a relationship is formed. Everyone understands what is happening and is thrilled!

It's almost too simple. Funny how it works that way.

NOW IT'S REAL

Just this week my mother filed for Social Security. Tough for me to process that...

Because I still remember mom from years ago. She was working hard in various jobs; up early in the morning for decades and doing work that other people wouldn't find glamorous. But those "off jobs", things like throwing morning newspapers or running a high school kitchen, always filled me with pride. Mom knows who she is. And from as early as I can remember, mom's number one priority was me and her other two kids. If that meant putting her own initiatives on the back-burner, that was fine. Mom's faith came first, family came next and her own agenda filled in the cracks.

Fast forward to mom turning 62 soon and ready to retire.

As you enter this next chapter of life mom, enjoy it. You deserve it.

I could provide a lot more color to this story, and would love to the next time we're together. But my point is: now... as my own mother files for Social Security & retires ... it becomes real. And no matter how many times I've helped you and my other friends and clients with retirement income strategies, nothing leaves a mark like a close-to-home experience.

So my challenge to you is this: **tell more personal stories**.

Think about times when it "became real" for you. Your family, your emotions, your bruises and scars, your life experiences. Then share those stories as often (more often than you are now) and "become real" to everyone listening to you. They all want to know who you are; so let them hear it.

CURSE OF BUSYNESS

Lights on, coffee started, computer up.

Email open, staff arrives, meetings begin.

More email responses, fire to put out, already lunchtime, huh?

Text from home, do you have a minute, what broke again?

Yes - my appointment arrived, that took longer than I thought, voicemails piled up.

Where'd everyone go?

Is it 6 already?

What did I get done today?

Don't fall prey to the curse of busyness. Busy is good. Busy is just. But busy can also be a 20th century-rooted "hard day's work". Because you, and only you, have control over your days. And I've met far too many professionals who are think busyness is the only way. It's not. In your heart of hearts I think you know that.

DOMINO DECISIONS

Coming back from an amazing week, I have 20+ action items swirling around my brain. Some are personal improvements, some professional, all impactful.

Been there?

So how do I tackle this? How do I jump into this list frantically and with passion, but still be smart about it? How do I make sure dust doesn't collect and luster doesn't fade on potential energy that needs my action? I'll tell you how... **3x5s, quick hits and dominos**.

1. 3×5 note cards
2. Quick Hits
3. Domino Decisions

First things first, get out your notes and a stack of **3×5 note cards**. *(Yes, I'm aware there are fancier, higher tech ways to do this, but this works incredibly well for me.)* On each 3×5 note card, take a permanent marker and write 1-3 key words on the front of the card, naming the idea you're taking action on. Then, on the back of that same card, take a pen and allow yourself up to 3 sentences to explain the idea in more detail.

Next, take those notecards (sometimes 20, sometimes 50) and divide them up into two piles. Pile one is **quick hits**. These are items that can be done now; or at least this week. Think fast, think one small change, one tweak, one minor improvement. But either you or someone on your team can crush this immediately.

The second pile of note cards are longer term initiatives. Some can be done this month, others this quarter and others this year or longer. Pile one, quick hits. Pile two, long(er) term.

Then take that longer term pile and order them from top to bottom, thinking about **Domino Decisions**. Which initiatives will have a reach into others further down the pile? Which order should you stack these – to have one action tip over the next, tipping over the next, tipping over the next?

Lastly, make just one pile of 3×5 note cards. Your quick hit list goes on top, domino decisions on the bottom. Each item is now peeled off, **one at a time**, and focused on until it's nailed and engrained. Your one-at-a-time focus makes 20 (or 50) tasks less daunting and more achievable. Don't think about the marathon, think about the next quarter mile. 105 quarter miles later and you're crossing the finish line.

The quick hits are done within the week, everyone sees immediate improvements, and then we move onto the fun stuff; the long game.

Steal this the next time you're flooded with ideas and overwhelmed with where to go. It's as easy as **3x5s, quick hits and dominos**. Then grab me with any improvements (as long as I get to keep my note cards).

CIRCLE OF ANXIETY

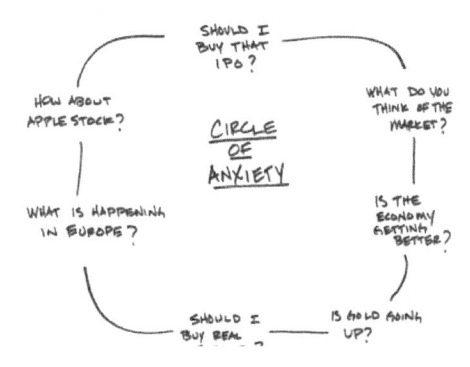

(Diagram: "CIRCLE OF ANXIETY" surrounded by questions: SHOULD I BUY THAT IPO? — WHAT DO YOU THINK OF THE MARKET? — IS THE ECONOMY GETTING BETTER? — IS GOLD GOING UP? — SHOULD I BUY REAL...? — WHAT IS HAPPENING IN EUROPE? — HOW ABOUT APPLE STOCK?)

Have you noticed how certain people tend to feel more anxiety than others? Why is that? Some people always seem so worried. What's happening with this crisis or that market? Who's coming into office? What's going on overseas? What if I do this? What if I do that?

I'm not saying those considerations aren't important. But I AM saying **most anxious people are focused on external forces**. What's going on outside of my control that's going to affect me? Anxious people believe the world happens to them.

But what about people who don't experience that same anxiety? What's happening in their mind? I'll submit that it's an entire different "self-talk". Want to lose the anxiety? Then focus on items within your control!

What can you do about the situation? What plan can you carry out? Who could you ask for advice? Where can you get the answer? What do you want to happen? And how do we get there?

Those anxious surroundings will never go away. They are constant. Forever. The difference is what you focus on. **The world doesn't happen to you. You happen to the world.**

Ringing in 2016 at Disney World

Evan's 1st day of Preschool

Meeting World Series Champion, Royals GM Dayton Moore

Granting a Wish Through Matt's Madness 2016

Honoring Lieutenant Michael P. Murphy - Completing Crossfit's 'Murph'

Father's Day 2016 with the Boys

Noah's 1st Day of Boy Scouts

Juneau, AK Dog Sledding with Mom on Mendenhall Glaicier

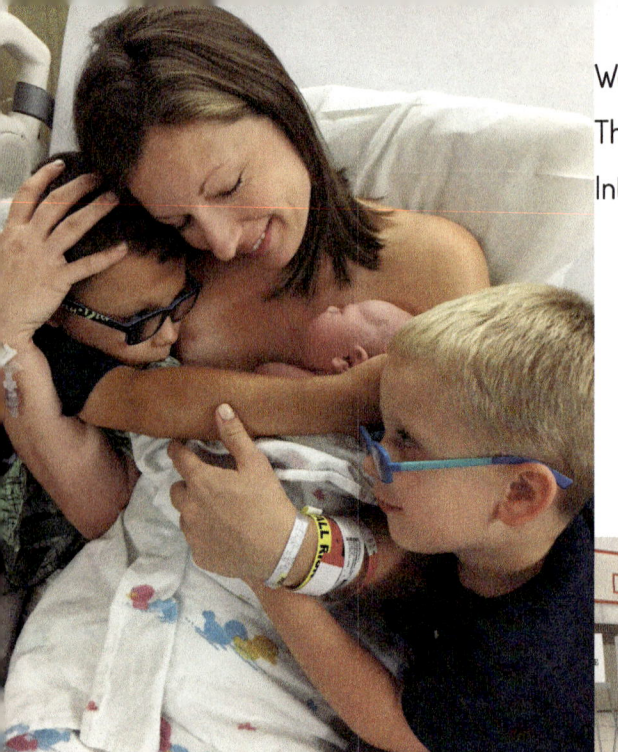

Welcoming Miracle #3 -
Theo Samuel Neuman -
Into our Family

Casting a Ballot in this Crazy Presidential Election

One Big, Happy, Loving, Fun, Laughing, We-Got-This Family

Water-themed Halloween Costumes (Sea Otter, Jacques Cousteau and Shark)

Parents, 3 boys, 3 sets of Godparents & a Priest Walk Into a Church.

CHAPTERS

Don't compare your **Chapter 1** to their **Chapter 20**. It's simply not fair *(to you)*.

"But Matt, that person [insert someone you admire] doesn't do that. Instead, they're focused on this item and that item moving forward. They haven't done (blank) in years!"

There's good reason for that. It's because (blank) was done by them years ago. Now it's so firmly ingrained in their hard wiring, in their team and in their structure that it's second nature. That was their chapter one, two or five. Now they're on chapter 20, which built on every chapter before.

Take the early or middle chapters out of *To Kill a Mockingbird* or *Huckleberry Finn* and the story ceases to exist. It can't be constructed and loses tone, context and staying power.

Don't compare your Chapter 1 to their Chapter 20. Instead, enjoy the chapter you're writing now and give it all you've got.

GOOD MANNERS

Coffee = **€1,50**

Coffee please **= €1.30**

Hello, coffee please **= €1**

Forget the financials of it, this menu dynamic sets an applaudable tone.

It's funny, it makes you smile and it carries a message. If you were sitting in this restaurant, it's clear what the owners **value** and **expect** from their customers. Plus, it's a **differentiator**.

In your world, how can you do the same thing?

DIRECTIONS

"When you get to the first stoplight, turn left. That's west I think. Yea, that's west. From there you'll want to go 4 blocks and hang a right on Oak Street. Take Oak a couple miles, probably 3 miles really once I think about it. You'll see a dry cleaner on your left and then you know you're almost there. Turn right just after that and look for the third office up the street. You're there!"

As soon as you said, "when you get to the first stoplight..." you lost me.

I'm going to plug the address into my phone GPS and do what it tells me. The last five minutes of your directions were appreciated for nicety and politeness – but honestly wasted time both of us will never get back. And now I also know you're still wired into the 1990s. At least you didn't hand me highlighted paper map!

We live in an economy flush with information. Power belongs to those who **know where to find it, can curate it and use it as needed**. Time to upgrade.

SILENCE IS AN ACTION

You either speak up or you don't. You either take action or stand stagnant. You either choose to move or cement yourself still. But everything is movement; one way or another.

Momentum's at work. Inertia's at work.

And since a choice is happening regardless; I'm choosing to speak up, to take action. I choose to charge ahead. You can do the same or you can stand silent, inactive and passive. But you're making that choice either way.

PUZZLE MASTER

* "A mutual fund here, a stock there. It's all diversified though; and we'd never pay more than 1% in fees."
* "I do some of our own stuff with Morningstar too."
* "Remember, we bought some bonds from a guy up the road a few years ago."
* "And most of our bank accounts have been with __ for years, but we do have these other couple banks for CDs."
* "Is our term life insurance still good? How long is that for?"
* "Someone told me I can get my 401(k) money now?"
* "I think we're good on long term care insurance. Our parents never really needed it."
* "We love our CPA. They know all the best ways to save us in taxes."
* "Yep. We have a will. Not sure about getting a trust though, seems like that's too much for us."

Sound familiar? Should I go on?

Your job is to take these statements and questions from your clients, and the dozens of others you hear over and over, **and make sense of them**.

Do you think the people you meet **want** six different, uncoordinated, professionals and ten different agendas in their financial life?

No. They want you. They want someone to take all the pieces and make sense of it. They want a puzzle master.

If you have a puzzle-solving process, that can be used every time for every

client, you win. Each puzzle will look different, and needs to be customized. But you have a process that works and is always improving.

If you don't, you'll be lost until you do. I'd start there.

JUST BECAUSE (GIFT)

We all appreciate gifts – birthday gifts, holiday gifts, congratulations gifts. But the downside of them is they're expected. Cakes, wrapping paper and the annual traditions seems to jade us a bit. So during those times, the "ordinary" gifts become forgotten, and even the unique and memorable ones fade away.

Tell me, what gift(s) did you receive for your birthday two years ago?

But then there's **"Just Because"** gifts. They show up for no reason, unexpectedly. Just like what I got in the mail today. It's a normal Monday, with no giftable holiday in sight. But the UPS package I got, from a business partner and very close friend, will leave an impression for a long time! *(As a matter of fact, there's a good chance I'm going to steal this idea and use it!)*

You couldn't do this better if you tried! The combination of Cathy's no-reason timing, personal story wrapped inside & very thoughtful words won't fade. Thank you Cathy.

Here, take a look:

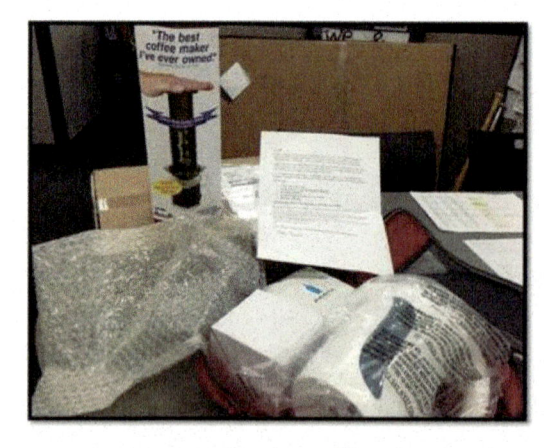

How could you use this? With clients? With friends? Who wouldn't appreciate a **"Just Because"** gift; with your personal story and thoughtful words inside?

Make this happen.

FORCED FOCUS

How many times are you working on something, and then get interrupted?

* Knock at the door
* Unexpected phone call
* Text message or
* (The worst) Email

Let me offer a solution that two people I trust, follow and admire have adopted to "forced focus".

First, there's Advisors Excel founder Cody Foster. I think Cody may have stolen this idea from Darren Hardy at one of his High Performance Forums. But regardless of the idea's genesis, it has a lot of merit. To show you a method behind Cody's "forced focus" I snuck into his office and snapped this picture:

Looking at that, **notice anything strange**??

You may have picked up on it, but look closely and you'll see Cody has two desks. One on the left for normal "work things" that require thought, focus and undivided attention. But then, did you notice the long desk on the right? Cody was gone the day I took this picture, but if he was inside the office you would've seen just one laptop computer plugged in on that right desk. And what's on that one laptop (and **NOT** on his desktop computer to the left)? Email.

Cody had email (which at the AE office averages 200 a day) taken completely off his normal computer. If he decides to tackle email, Cody needs to physically walk over to another desk, stand there since there's no chair, and go through his inbox.

* Do you think he lets email get in the way of bigger objectives?
* How would this same set up in your office change focus?

Next, there's Austin Kleon – author of *Steal Like an Artist*, which is **the book I've gifted more than any YTD**. Austin's forced focus comes in the form of two desks also, but in a different way. Here's a pic to explain:

On his two desk setup, Austin says:

"I have two desks in my office — one's "analog" and one's "digital." The analog desk has nothing but markers, pens, pencils, paper, and newspaper. Nothing electronic is allowed on the desk — this is how I keep myself off Twitter, etc. This is where most of my work is born. The digital desk has my laptop, my monitor, my scanner, my Wacom tablet, and a MIDI keyboard controller for if I want to record any music. (Like a lot of writers, I'm a wannabe musician.) This is where I edit, publish, etc."

Could you, or anyone else in your office, employ this strategy too? Anyone who needs to stay right-brained would love this feel – giving them permission to be creative, without electronic distraction!

There are countless other ways to force your own focus – I'm simply highlighting two

I love. If you have others that work for you, I'd love to hear them! And if you decide to set up your office/desk(s) like Cody or Austin above, you've got to share that with me too!

Stay focused; whatever that means, however that works for you.

CELEBRATE IT ALL

It's time you start celebrating things. Big things, small things, short things, tall things (too much Dr. Seuss at home?!?). Time to start celebrating milestones, improvements, and successes of all kinds, more often. Celebrate it all.

In the office:
* Celebrate best months of all time – every time, every month.
* Celebrate staff hiring anniversaries *(would it be crude to celebrate firing anniversaries?)*.
* Celebrate successful workshops and client events.
* Celebrate the "wrong" clients who didn't partner with your firm.

At home:
* Celebrate books you finish reading.
* Celebrate during the trips you get to take.
* Celebrate giving back, charity and all the impact you make.
* Celebrate family dinners together.

For yourself:

* Celebrate half birthdays. (Like my son Noah, turning 6 ½ with his **"py Day ah!"** €cake. Or the late, no question, most accomplished coach of all time John Wooden – who according to my friend Don Yaeger, celebrated half birthdays late into his 90s!)
* Celebrate Personal Records (PRs) of any kind – weight, strength, charity or clarity.
* Celebrate 15 minutes of silence.
* Celebrate whatever makes you smile.

Why celebrate so much?

One, because it's fun and what's the alternative? Two, because everyone around you will be happier and deserves it. Third, because you work too hard to not enjoy it.

Now go celebrate something. Anything.

USELESS PLASTIC CRAP

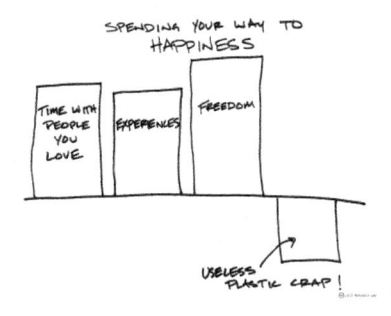

[Hand-drawn bar chart titled "SPENDING YOUR WAY TO HAPPINESS" showing bars labeled "TIME WITH PEOPLE YOU LOVE", "EXPERIENCES", "FREEDOM", and a downward bar labeled "USELESS PLASTIC CRAP!"]

Earlier I wrote something called "Money Makes You..." which is now one of my most viewed posts yet. The positive feedback was overwhelming.

In short, I was reminiscing about the last 10 years with my close friend Sandy; especially some lifelong lessons I've learned from her, including that:

"To Sandy, money:
1. Gives you comfort
2. Gives you choices
3. And beyond that – **money makes you more of who you are**
4. If you're greedy, money will make you more so.
5. If you're unethical, money will bend those rules further.
6. If you're grateful, that spirit of love and gratitude will shine brighter.
7. If you're giving, your reach will grow wider and deeper.
8. If you're self-centered, your focus will heighten inward.
9. If your values are centered on family or faith; possessions or recognition, they will strengthen regardless.

Money makes you more of who you are."

But notice in that post, I didn't talk about what you spend your money on. That's for today. And that's simple. If you agree with me (and Sandy) that money makes you more of who you are; then let's make sure we're consumed with worthwhile pursuits.

Moving forward, let's spend our way to more time with people we love.

Moving forward, let's spend our way to be in the middle of more life experiences.

Moving forward, let's spend our way to more freedom.

Moving forward, let's quit spending our money on useless plastic crap.

Money gives you more comfort and choices then it makes you more of who you are. Be decisive on that last part.

3 YEARS FROM NOW

"3 years from now, will it even matter?"

Whatever you're worrying about, thinking on, those items that keep running through your head, 100 miles per hour today. 3 years from now, will they matter?

Because 3 years ago, you were making a lot of decisions that are inconsequential today.

Some of those presentations, meetings, "fires," tasks and problems mean nothing. But they meant the world to you then.

If you decide **"Yes. This will matter."** Then take a deep breath and focus. Control what you can control, make a confident decision and build on it.

If you decide **"No. This isn't important."** Then let it go. Either let that work move to another person in your circle or set it loose entirely.

"3 years from now, will this even matter?" It puts a lot into perspective.

IS VULNERABILITY WEAK?

Short and sweet today. Here's a *(paraphrased, but close to exact)* quote I heard today, from a very successful financial advisor in my office:

"As an advisor, I've always been taught to think that vulnerability meant weakness. What I've learned today is that vulnerability is relatability...and relatability is where connections are forged.

We've been taught all wrong in this industry. We prop ourselves up with "credentials" and "accolades" and "expertise." People don't connect to me because of the letters after my name.

When it comes to people, **TRUST** *is more powerful than knowledge. People don't initially* **TRUST** *me because I know things. They* **TRUST** *me because they can* **RELATE** *to me."*

If your next prospect meets you, then meets him – who do they choose?

PATH TO MASTERY

There's a real-life path to mastery. And it hurts. And it's ugly. People don't like it and very few people will ever achieve it. It goes something like this:

This is hard.
(If it were easy, wouldn't everyone do it?)

I don't **feel** like doing _____ today.
(Neither does anyone else. So you can either join them or do it regardless of how you feel.)

Everyone else has more time than me.
(To do what? Watch TV? Hang out at the bar? Sleep in until 9 or 10 am? If you want to master something, you'll make time.)

I don't **feel** like this is making a difference.
(You could go by feelings again and give up like everyone else. Or you could trust the process & all your hard work up to now.)

Almost no one else is doing this.

(And now you're getting somewhere!)

Along your path to mastery (of any subject) it's helpful to give yourself instructions:

1. Talk to yourself, instead of listening to yourself.
2. Ask the question, "What is one thing I can do to make the situation better?" Rather than, "Why is this happening to me?"
3. Live by principles rather than feelings.

There. You have it.

Now what are you going to do with it?

*Huge thanks to my friend Joshua Medcalf for sharing this insight with me. I was able to meet Joshua recently, while simultaneously reading his book **Burn Your Goals**. If you haven't already, check this man out.

IT'S EASY

It's easy to turn on the television.

It's easy to just run through the drive-thru.

It's easy to sleep in.

It's easy to not work out.

It's easy to complain, assume malice, blame external and never look internal. But what are you **willing to do that's hard**?

Listening to Shay Carl (From Manual Laborer to 2.3 Billion YouTube Views) today, his quote stuck with me, *"Work will work when nothing else will work."*

Let's make it happen.

BROTHER IN LAW ADVICE

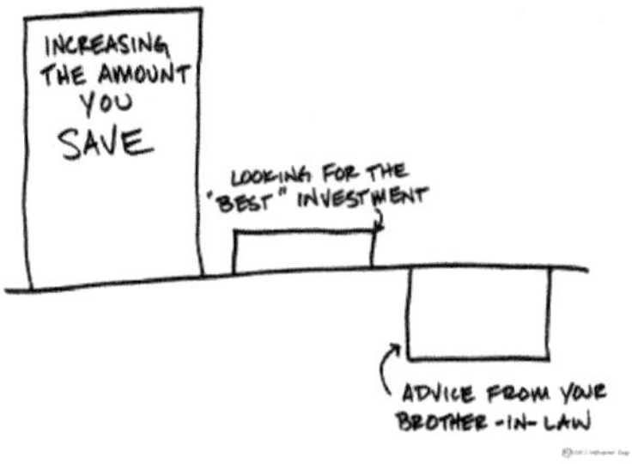
INCREASING THE AMOUNT YOU SAVE
LOOKING FOR THE "BEST" INVESTMENT
ADVICE FROM YOUR BROTHER-IN-LAW

Even though we intellectually know what matters, why do we waste so much energy on things that don't?

How much time have you spent talking about how much to save?

What about your investment options?

What about an idea your brother in law (or golfing buddy or co-worker or that guy at the gym) told you about?

We concentrate in the wrong places, it's human nature. But to get where you want to go, we have to fight it.

IDENTITY

There's a problem with winning.

Winning the contest, winning the war or winning the sale all come at a cost. The problem is what's next? And with winning, you always need **more** to feel that same accomplishment. Without the next win, we're lost.

If you're a *"somebody"* when you fight and win, what are you when you fight and lose? I hope that answer doesn't define you.

If I asked, **"who would you be if you weren't a financial professional?"** I'd hear things like a pilot, a musician, an attorney or a restaurant owner. But I didn't ask **what** you would be, I asked **who**. What you do and who you are should be different answers. Yet for a lot of us, those two things become interchangeable, and again our identity becomes only what we do.

As a genuine professional, loved family leader and authentic member of multiple communities, define yourself differently. When someone asks you what you do, respond with things you enjoy doing, respond with your passions. And for the sake of everyone's identity, **PLEASE stop asking others what they do for a living (as if that's most important)**. Instead, ask
* What makes them smile every day?
* What are they passionate about?
* What do they look forward to the most when they wake up?

Define identity in yourself and others differently from today forward.

8 AM EMAIL

Is there anything worse than 8 am email?

How frustrating, even more... how de-motivating, is looking at email to start your day? I don't know who said it, but a long time ago I heard:

"Email is someone else's ultimate to do list".

So don't do it! Don't start your day with **reactive** work, that someone else *(internal or external)* put on your computer screen. Do something different. Create something different.

What if instead you:
1. Didn't open email until 10 am, or noon, or even later every day?
2. Had one staff member who signed a confidentiality agreement and took over your email *(briefing you on a need-to-know basis)*?
3. Time-Blocked specific hours each day *(or days each week)* to check email, turning it off all other times?
4. Moved email to a secondary computer, where you had to consciously move to be in front of it?

Because this isn't about email or not – since we know it's required on some level. Instead, this is about **proactive vs. reactive, conscious vs. unconscious, creating vs. managing, their to-do list vs. yours.**

You can quit 8 am email tomorrow, and the next, the next, and every day after that. If you want to.

HAVE VS. GET

Recently I was headed to an industry training, hoping to network with friends and colleagues; hoping to become better and light a fire in my belly. Packing the night before, and casually visiting with my wife, she asked a couple polite questions about the event. I said,

"I'm headed to Atlanta. I have to attend this conference."

And in saying that, I noticed negativity in my own voice. Soon after that came out of my mouth, it hit me. I don't **have** to attend this conference. I **get** to attend.

Important distinction.

How many other professionals would jump at the chance to attend this event? And pay handsomely to do it? I was surrounding myself with incredible professionals, catching up with friends and become better at my craft. Perspective.

The first expression (*"I have to..."*) is a language of obligation. Nothing wrong with obligation or accountability. But a lot of times, "I have to..." becomes negative. It becomes the language of a victim who's lost control and is being forced to do something.

The second expression (*"I get to..."*) confers empowerment. When you get to do something, you're privileged and you're coming from a place of positivity and opportunity. The change is one word, but it's enormous.

I don't have to workout at 5AM, I get to. My body and mind are healthy enough to take on the physical activity and consequential benefits.

I don't have to be in the office today, I get to. I'm privileged to visit with team members and partners all day who care what I have to say.

I don't have to spend time reading the Word today, I get to. What a gift to have an element of faith in my life that serves as a guiding light.

I don't have to straighten things at home tonight, I get to. I'm incredibly blessed to live where I do, with who I do, in the manner I do.

Now it's your turn. Today you **get** to change one word and add perspective to your life.

THE LINE BETWEEN

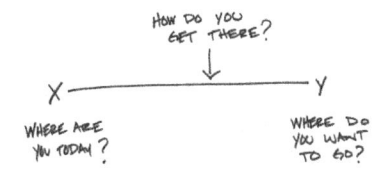

Diagram: X (Where are you today?) ——— Y (Where do you want to go?), with arrow labeled "How do you get there?"

This is a straightforward one to understand.

Informed = Calm
Uninformed = Anxious

Take this whatever direction you want.
* Become more informed yourself, and you're more calm with clients.
* Clients become more informed about their retirement income plan, and they're more calm and feel more confident about their retirement strategies.
* Prospects become more informed about your process, and they're more calm about making a decision to work with you.
* Your kids are more informed about family finances, and they're more calm about your financial future.
* Your staff is more informed about your expectations, and they're more calm about achieving goals.
* On ... and on ... and on.

Figure out what you, your clients, your family and your team are most anxious about, them help them become more informed. Now we're talking.

4 STEP MARKETING

1. Step One: Invent something worth making & worth talking about. You need to be proud of it. And it needs to bring more than marginal change.

2. Step Two: Build your "something" in a way people clearly benefit. Will they get excited?

3. Step Three: Tell your story. Do this in front of the right people in the right way.

4. Step Four *(the hardest)*: Show up consistently, open-minded and strong-willed. Generously lead others as you collectively build confidence.

FOMO

FO·MO / ˈfômô/ *Noun informal*

> early 21st century: abbreviation of **fear of missing out**.
> anxiety that an exciting or interesting event may currently be happening elsewhere, often aroused by posts seen on a social media website.

It's Monday night, 9:30 pm and I'm in Nashville. Next to the Grand Ole' Opry, I'm walking inside a monstrosity of a hotel named the Gaylord Opryland. Ever been there? Think 2800 rooms, 15 restaurants, indoor boat rides, an on-site golf course and 700,000 square feet of event space. Insane.

Walking back to my room, trying to not get lost, I come across a friend of mine (let's call him Joe). With a beer in his hand and a look in his eye, Joe asks me:

"Matt, you going to bed?".

"Yep. Got an early morning working out and then into our event, so it's my time," I reply.

"I don't know what I'm going to do," Joe blurted out, verbalizing his internal dialogue. That much was very obvious. You could literally see the wheels turning inside his skull. "I need to go to bed too, but I'm afraid of missing out."

"Missing out on what?" I sincerely asked. Maybe I'd missed something happening.

"Nothing really," he replied. "But who knows what might happen. I mean, people are still at the bar and I want to be there if something happens. You know, a

FOMO kinda thing..."

We talked for another minute and then I headed towards my room, while Joe shuffled the opposite way towards the bar. But the entire walk back to my room, I kept thinking – **FOMO. Fear of Missing Out. How does that make sense**?

Because the question isn't "Am I missing out?". Let me solve that for you. Yes. Yes, you're missing out. Yes, you're missing out on something right now. You're missing out on nearly everything that exists right now, except this tiny little sliver of a moment you're choosing to be part of. And for every "Yes, I want to be part of that ..." decision, you're exchanging every other alternative. It's not good or bad in isolation. It's a fact.

So are you choosing to be here or there? With that person or this? Focused on objective one or two? NOT "Am I missing out?". Fear of Missing Out – that's ridiculous.

The next morning I was up early and worked out as planned, ate healthy and was ready to learn by 8. My friend never spoke of working out, ate a not-so-healthy last minute breakfast, was a few minutes late and groggy until noon. This is not a "good or bad" comparison though, with anyone making superior choices. Were we both part of something? Yes. Did we both miss out on something? Yes. Because again, none of those results are good or bad in isolation. But...

I hope Joe found what he wanted in Nashville. I did. And most importantly, I hope neither of us missed out on the wrong thing.

MAJORING IN THE MINORS

You could be the best proofreader in your office. Or the firm's database IT expert. Or the division's paperwork perfectionist, confirmation call royalty or the most decorated tax specialist this side of the Mississippi.

And if those are your passions, great. Run with them! Love your work and know you found your calling.

But for the majority of you, I know they're not.

Proofreading, databases, IT, paperwork, standard calls and tax law. Those things are good, those things are important. But they're **"minors"**. In your world, those details can be hired for or outsourced to experts; to people (believe it or not) who are much better than you at them. Those staff people or outsourced partners can major in those minors, giving you freedom.

While you're a small, lean and growing firm, you take on a lot of tasks. That's part of the fun and learning experience. We get that. But as you grow in awareness and influence, things have to evolve. I visit with firms grossing half a million, $1 million, $5 million, $10 million+ a year in revenue , and it's amazing how many are still operating like the good 'ole start-up days. Is it a **lack of vision**? An **ego** thing? A **control** thing? I'm not a psychologist and don't play one on TV. I'm not sure.

But as you become more successful, don't let the **"minor"** tasks *scare* you away from oing **"major"** work.

Major in the majors. The world needs your contribution there.

REVERSE ENGINEERING

I bet we do it different.

I don't know why, because I've never thought this way. But most people do. I bet you look at things like this:
* **STEP 1:** Here's where I am today
* **STEP 2:** And if I do ____ for ____ weeks/months/years
* **STEP 3:** Here's where I'll be

But my mind doesn't work like that. Never has.

I have to **reverse engineer** into just about everything *(sometimes driving people around me, including my wife, nuts)*!

I tell myself:
* **STEP 1:** Here's where I want to be
* **STEP 2:** Here's where I am today
* **STEP 3:** And if I do ____ for ____ weeks/months/years (I'm there)!

Again, I don't know why I do that. I only know I'm wired that way and it works for me. Maybe you can steal that sometime and use it too...

STICKER (& REFERRAL) SHOCK

It's a sunny, Sunday afternoon and I'm walking through a scenic outdoor shopping area in Kansas City. We stroll past store-after-store and as we cross Brooks Brothers, I decide to walk in. As you'd expect, 20 feet into the store a salesperson approaches and I explain I'm "just looking". *(Completely unrelated note, how many times has he heard "Just looking..."? That's gotta get old. He really needs to change his approach.)*

While browsing around Brooks Brothers, I end up buying two pairs of dress pants. Nice pants, fair price, no big deal. A regular purchase and something I was happy with. Everything status quo.

Getting back home, I tried these pants on again and it was definite; they'd need some minor alternations done. Bring the hem up, take the waist in, let the thighs out. Again, status quo. Picking up my cell phone I Google and call a local men's store, to ask if they'd alter these pairs of pants for me.

"Sorry sir, we don't do alterations in store. But I can give you the person who does it for us."

"Sure," I respond, ready to get this done. "Who's that? And what's the number?"

"It's (785) 843-xxxx and be sure to tell them we sent you. She's done a great job for us for years."

Fast forward a couple days and I'm in a nice woman's home alteration room.

She's nice, professional and you can tell has done this for years, just like the men's store said. She chalks a few lines, pins a couple others and I'm gone. Third time, status quo and everything's good.

Where's this headed?

A week later, I'm back at this nice woman's home to get the pants and be on my way. Taking the two pairs of pants, I ask her, *"How much do I owe you?"*.

Seemingly without rhyme or reason, without calculation or reflection she responds, "$71.50".

"$71.50? I just had the two pairs of pants, right?"

"Right. $35 apiece and a little extra for tax."

I reach into my wallet, hand her $75 and tell her to keep the change. Then I walk out the front door and ask myself – **what just happened**? You'll have to remember, I live in Kansas. Not New York, not San Francisco, not Chicago. Did she just charge me more because the pants were from a nice store? Did she notice a nice car I was driving? Was she in a bad mood and took it out on me? Or does she really charge $35 for every pair of pants and half hour's work?

The point being...
This has zero to do about the money. It's the principle. While I'd rather pay less than more, I understand quality comes at a premium. But the price I was charged was never communicated and wildly out of range with my expectations.

My question to you; do your clients ever feel that way?

* **Step 1** – Status quo, they're relatively happy *(they "buy the pants")*.
* **Step 2** – Status quo, things move forward like they expect *(they "need to get alterations")*.
* **Step 3** – Status quo, work happens, timelines are met, referrals are made *(they "get fitted")*.
* **Step 4** – It blows up. Follow through is lacking, discomfort outweighs value, love is lost and client turn from lifelong fans to resentful antagonists *(they "pay too much")*.

There's no happy ending to this story. I never went back to that tailor. I've never again set foot into that men's store who made the referral. I'll remember next time to ask how much something costs.

Make sure this never happens in your world. Clean up your processes from start to finish, and focus on the end as much as the beginning! Clients need and deserve that; otherwise they'll never come back for more.

CANCELLATION BLISS

You know when something's on your calendar, and looking at it, your shoulders sink? You frown, roll your eyes or shake your head? That activity sucks the spirit out of your day.

"Why do I schedule things like that?" is your internal dialogue.

Then ... the **appointment cancels**. Or no shows.

And instead of feeling like you lost something; you feel **relief**. Call it **cancellation bliss**. Shoulders raise, frowns reverse, eyes stop rolling, heads stop shaking and life is breathed back into your day. Exhale.

That leaves you with the next hour freed up. What should you do with it? A million things pull at your time, but let me offer the best solution – best now, and best long term.

Whatever that cancelled activity was, the thing that just gave you relief and bliss, **get rid of it forever**. Do whatever's necessary to get that off your calendar. Delegate, consolidate, modify or delete. But never again see that item on your calendar and feel what you did before the cancellation.

You created this business for a reason. Own your calendar and decisions.

TRUST THE (CAKE-MAKING) PROCESS

A week earlier we'd welcomed our third son into the world...

I was at home, transitioning into the "new normal". Diapers, nap cycles, shorter nights, longer smiles. And alongside me was a recovering, healthy, happy, beautiful wife; along with two boys in school (1st grade & preschool) and now boy #3 – Theo Samuel! Life. Is. Good.

But being at home that long, something funny happened. **I got stir crazy.**
So one afternoon I told my wife, "I'm gonna bake a cake."

To which she smirked and cautioned me. You could tell Alice thought I was nuts. Beyond pancakes, eggs and warming up leftovers I wasn't much for cooking.

I had a Paleo cookbook in front of me that included ingredients I didn't know and words I didn't understand. But the picture looked good and I'd decided, I wanted to do this. And when I say *"bake a cake"* I'm not talking about something simple. I'm talking about triple layer, no processed sugar or dairy, buttercream icing, ganache (see, I learned a new word) – all from scratch. Hours were in front of me. If we're gonna do it, let's do it. Hearing and seeing all this, my wife just smiled.

Thinking back on it, I really didn't care about baking a cake, **I wanted to learn something new**. Even if it was inside my own kitchen, I wanted something I'd never done before that was challenging. In front of me was the step-by-step ingredients and directions. All I needed to do was follow through. So what happened? You can probably guess...

I messed up. More than once. Wrong ingredient, forgotten step, and I still can't understand why the cookbook said "60 minutes prep time" total & it took me over 2 hours!

Moving into the early evening, my wife came back into the kitchen; but this time she smiled a different smile. To her surprise, something smelled good and looked above average. **Really? Did Matt do that?!?** Alice was even texting my sister in amazement about what she was witnessing. And that night for dinner (plus multiple times that week), our family of five dug into the cake. Success!

Since then, I've been cooking a little more. Everything I see doesn't feel half as challenging as that cake. Week after week, dinners become more "doable" and I can repeat items quicker and more efficient. There's still a long way to go, but I picked up a new skill and confidence level that'll carry into the future.

So ask yourself – **When was the last time you learned something new?** Something you could follow step-by-step the first time and screw things up, but still get to the finish line. Then continue to repeat it with more precision. **Is it time to challenge yourself again?** Because Lord knows, if I can bake that cake from scratch, you can do almost anything.

GET BUSY

You don't complain when you're doing productive work. When you found a state of flow and making an impact in a big way.

Impact leads to contribution leads to fulfillment.

But ask someone how they're doing and you're bound to hear *"fine", "good"* or ***"busy"*** 90% of the time.

- Busy is mind-numbing.
- Busy is tiresome.
- Busy sucks the enthusiasm out.
- **Busy is the opposite of produc**
- **tive**.

So let's vow to erase that old adage of "Get Busy" from our mindsets forever. Let's get productive.

WALKING INTO THE (CO) SUNSET

Let me share **one of the most rewarding emails I've received in my career**.

It comes from Jim in Houston. Jim's a long-time, loyal client of mine (since 2008) and an even better friend. I admire and respect Jim on every level; as he's brought a lot to my life. Here's what Jim had to say:

From: Jim
Sent: Wednesday, September 07, 2016 3:25 PM
To: Matt Neuman
Subject: Re: Video postponement

... Everything came together creating the perfect time.

I'm 51, having done this 20 yrs, invested well along the way, created a nice biz to sell and I don't really need to work any longer. I'm a fiduciary advisor with a clean 20 yr history of helping clients and decided that in lieu of the day to day of running a financial services business is no longer fun. And last year was my 12th consecutive year of increasing revenue. Last year was almost $1M in revenue. So, for me to walk away now, should tell you that I don't enjoy this anymore.

I did a T-square on selling and going to CO or keeping on here in Houston. Overwhelmingly, it was to sell and get to CO as soon as I can. Most likely, I'll go away, write a book, then resurface in the life market in a state with four seasons... Jim

Wow.

Powerful.

Inspiring.

Hopefully Jim's email triggers reflection in your mind. How well are you investing along the way? Are you creating something to sell? Is your record staying clean? And most importantly, are you creating a practice that is fun & enjoyable?

I take no credit for Jim's success and ultimate (at least for now) retirement at 51. He's the catalyst, decision maker and hero of this story.

But I'd be lying to say it wasn't fulfilling to know Jim & I have walked side-by-side for 8 of those last 12 increasing revenue years. We were working together in 2010, when Jim decided to quit selling commissioned securities, and build a practice he could later sell. Jim also found the partner to sell his practice to through our connections. Those small roles I played are **why I do what I do**. That's why Jim's story is so rewarding and fulfilling on my level.

Enjoy your walk into the Colorado sunset Jim (& Lorri). Remember us on whatever path you take in this next season. And one more time, for choosing me and AE – thank you.

WANT VS. NEED

WANT to make more money? Might happen. Probably not.

WANT to get fit? Good luck.

WANT a better relationship with your spouse? Sure.

But…

NEED to clear another $3k/month or lose your house? Let's do this.

NEED to drop 20 pounds or risk a stroke? 100% done.

NEED to focus on your spouse or they're gone? Forever? You'll do the work.

WANT vs. NEED.

That's a big difference, in your motivation and *psyche*. Now use it to your advantage.

LET'S GET THIS

1st – Let's get this **verbalized**.
2nd – Let's get this **launched**.
3rd – Let's get this **working**.
4th – Let's get this **effective**.
5th – Let's get this **efficient**.
6th – Let's get this **beautiful**.
7th – Let's get this **simplified**.
8th – Let's get this **automated**.

Let's start again.

WORTHLESS WEATHER

What is it about the weather that somehow "controls" our day?
- Sunny day = Great, let's get something done!
- Cloudy day = Hunker down.
- Rain or Snow = Not this again, let's just get through it.
- Cold = Slow or Hot = Fast.

What if we **refused** to let an external condition like the weather affect our mood or attitude ever again?
Better yet, what if we became counter-cultural to this?
Embrace the difference. Do what others don't. Become conditioned to you being the driving factor that effects your mood, attitude, performance and

output – not something as trivial as the weather. **Internal vs. External.** And the next time it rains or snows... step outside and smile.

FINAL THOUGHTS

Most can agree the financial advisory world is filled with empty promises and shiny objects. That's due in part to the quick-start mentality of most financial advisors who are disposed to ready-fire-aim. That's also due to opportunistic vendors and "service providers" who play into that mentality, in hopes of turning a quick buck. These factors have created a world of "easy money" and "silver bullets" where it's easy to lose sight of reality.

That's why *On Matthew's Mind* was created and has taken off; to bring reality back to your world. A reality that knows prosperity doesn't include shortcuts. The closest thing you'll find to shortcuts are proven ideas with strings attached, specifically strings of vulnerability and focus. These ideas have launched others from Point A to Point B (wherever those respective points are) in their lives and have the potential to do the same for you.

Peers, mentors and teachers have been where you want to go. Find out what's worked for them and what hasn't. What do they think about in the morning? What decisions have they made that you can gather wisdom from? What took them 5 years to capitalize on, that empowered with this knowledge may only take you 3 months? And most importantly, what can you take from this work, and internalize into your own world to make a lasting impact on yourself and others?

My challenge is to take this collection, these best practices, and use them as a springboard. The most successful financial advisors in the country have opened their minds and right now you're holding those thoughts. *On Matthew's Mind* will shorten your learning curve and give you internal permission to have more, serve more, and be more.